DECLUTTER YOUR LIFE

------ ❦❦❦❦ ------

How to organize a clean home, a clear mind and be on your way to success

Chris S Jennings

© Copyright 2019 by Chris S Jennings - All rights reserved.

The follow book is reproduced below with the goal of providing information that is as accurate and reliable as possible. Regardless, purchasing this book can be seen as consent to the fact that both the publisher and the author of this book are in no way experts on the topics discussed within and that any recommendations or suggestions that are made herein are for entertainment purposes only. Professionals should be consulted as needed prior to undertaking any of the action endorsed herein.

This declaration is deemed fair and valid by both the American Bar Association and the Committee of Publishers Association and is legally binding throughout the United States.

Furthermore, the transmission, duplication or reproduction of any of the following work including specific information will be considered an illegal act irrespective of if it is done electronically or in print. This extends to creating a secondary or tertiary copy of the work or a recorded copy and is only allowed with express written consent from the Publisher. All additional right reserved.

The information in the following pages is broadly considered to be a truthful and accurate account of facts and as such any inattention, use or misuse of the information in question by the reader will render any resulting actions solely under their purview. There are no scenarios in which the publisher or the original author of this work can be in any fashion deemed liable for any hardship or damages that may befall them after undertaking information described herein.

Additionally, the information in the following pages is intended only for informational purposes and should thus be thought of as universal. As befitting its nature, it is presented without assurance regarding its prolonged validity or interim quality. Trademarks that are mentioned are done without written consent and can in no way be considered an endorsement from the trademark holder.

Your Free Gift

As a way of saying thank you for your purchase, I wanted to offer you a free bonus e-book called **3 Incredible Life Changing Daily Habits That Can Help You To Heal Any Pain In Your Life**

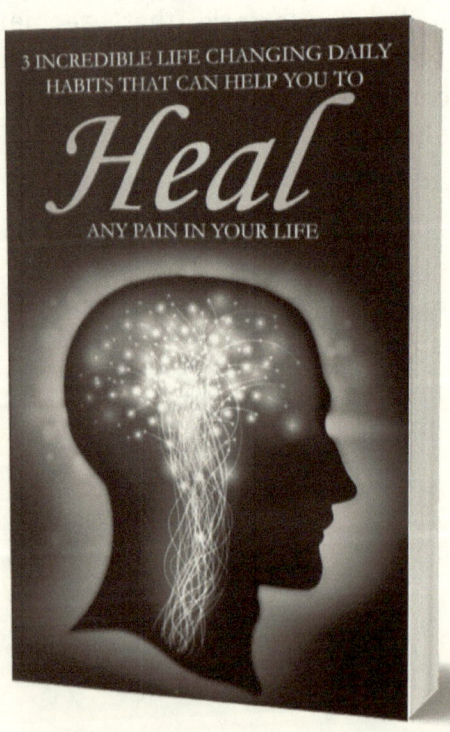

Download the free ebook here: https://www.subscribepage.com/healing

Are you tired of letting your negative emotions consume you? Life throws a lot of curveballs at us: illness, abandonment, death, heartbreak, injury, the list goes on. We have found 3 scientifically endorsed daily habits that can significantly help you to heal any emotional pain and help take back control for you to start living a more positive life right now.

Listen to this book for free

Do you want to be able to listen to this book whenever you want? Maybe whilst driving to work or running errands. It can be difficult nowadays to sit down and listen to a book. So I am really excited to let you know that this book is available in audio format. What's great is you can get this book for FREE as part of a 30-day audible trial. Thereafter if you don't want to stay an Audible member you can cancel, but keep the book.

Benefits of signing up to audible:

- After the trial, you get 1 free audiobook and 2 free audio originals each month
- Can roll over any unused credits
- Choose from over 425,000 + titles
- Listen anywhere with the Audible app and across multiple devices
- Keep your audiobooks forever, even if you cancel your membership

Click below to get started

Audible US - https://tinyurl.com/y6j5ofez

Audible UK - https://tinyurl.com/y52nhzgk

Audible FR - https://tinyurl.com/y2lznbj7

Audible DE- https://tinyurl.com/yy3emd3d

TABLE OF CONTENTS

INTRODUCTION 1

CHAPTER 1: THE POWER OF DECLUTTERING 3

- You Will Feel a Greater Sense of Vibrancy 3
- Your Schedule Will Clear Up, Big Time 4
- You Begin To Move Forward In Life 6
- You Can Address Your Personal Issues 7
- Your Habits Can Be Transformed 8
- You Feel More Rested and Less Stressed 9

CHAPTER 2: DECLUTTERING YOUR MINDSET 11

- Identifying Your Core Values 12
- Overcoming Procrastination 14
- Releasing Negative Thought Patterns 17
- Increasing Your Mental Resiliency 18

CHAPTER 3: DECLUTTERING YOUR HOME 21

- How to Tackle the Decluttering of your Home 22
- Decluttering Your Bedroom 22
  - *Eliminate Unwanted Clothes* 23
  - *Use Your Hamper* 23
  - *Use Containers to Contain the Clutter* 23
  - *Organize Your Closet* 24
  - *Use Minimalistic Decorations* 24
- Decluttering Your Kitchen 24
  - *Eliminate the Excess Junk* 25
  - *Keep Your Counters Clear* 25
  - *Use Storage Solutions for Cleaner Drawers and Cupboards* 25
  - *Build a Communications Center* 26
  - *Clean Out Underneath Your Sink* 26
  - *Clean Out Your Food Supply* 26
- Decluttering Your Living Room 27
  - *Return Everything to Where It Belongs* 27
  - *Use A Declutter Basket* 27
  - *Organize Your Media Cabinet* 28
  - *Minimize Your Decorations* 28
- Decluttering Your Bathrooms 28
  - *Eliminated Unwanted Products* 29
  - *Clean Absolutely Everything Off* 29

Use Effective Storage Solutions 29
DECLUTTERING STORAGE 29
Commit To Going through Everything 30
Use Labeled Bins 30
Keep the Space Clean 31

CHAPTER 4: DECLUTTERING YOUR FINANCES 33

MASTERING THE ART OF BUDGETING 34
RELEASING FINANCIAL BURDENS YOU DON'T NEED 36
HAVING WEEKLY SPENDING LIMITS 37
TAKING THE OCCASIONAL CASH FREEZE BREAK 38

CHAPTER 5: DECLUTTERING YOUR RELATIONSHIPS 41

IDENTIFYING CLUTTER IN YOUR SOCIAL CIRCLE 42
REMOVING TOXIC RELATIONSHIPS FROM YOUR LIFE 44
Be Completely Honest From the Start 45
Avoid Playing the Blame Game 45
End the Relationship Completely 46
CLEANING UP YOUR SOCIAL MEDIA 47
BEING MORE PRESENT AT THE MOMENT 48
MAKING TIME FOR THE ONES YOU LOVE 50

CHAPTER 6: HEALTHY HABITS FOR DECLUTTERING 53

TAKE THINGS SLOWLY, THERE IS NO RUSH 53
BE PRACTICAL ABOUT WHAT YOU CAN ACHIEVE 54
DO NOT BE AFRAID TO ASK FOR SUPPORT 55
TAKE BEFORE AND AFTER PHOTOGRAPHS 56
BE COMPASSIONATE WITH YOURSELF 57
MAKE IT A FUN EXPERIENCE 58
USE A QUARANTINE PRACTICE IF YOU NEED TO 59
LOOK AT THE POSITIVE SIDE OF THINGS 60
BEGIN BUILDING MORE POSITIVITY INTO YOUR LIFE 61

CONCLUSION 63

INTRODUCTION

Congratulations on downloading ***Declutter!***

Over the next six chapters, you are going to be guided on a journey of how you can declutter your life and your home one step at a time. This journey can be a trying one, but it is also highly rewarding and stands to offer you many great benefits along the way. From having a stronger sense of mental clarity and wellbeing to feeling better about your home, there are many benefits that you gain when you focus on decluttering your life.

As you go through this journey, I encourage you to really embrace the act of compassion and understanding. The fact that you have chosen to invest in learning more about the process of decluttering proves that you are serious about making meaningful changes in your life. It also suggests that you may have attempted to do it on your own but found that you were left feeling overwhelmed or at a loss for where to start or what to do. This feeling of frustration and confusion is completely natural, and you are not alone in feeling it. In fact, *most* people feel that way when they begin decluttering their lives and homes! Being compassionate and understanding with yourself and not judging yourself for any feelings that may come up along the way will ensure that you are able to continue along with the process of decluttering.

This book has been designed in a step-by-step process, starting with your mind and leading you to the point of decluttering your social circle and friendships. By following this book in the order it has been presented to you with, you can equip yourself with the necessary resources to successfully achieve each successive step. Attempting to do too much at once or skip over steps could result in an increase in overwhelm and a decreased likelihood of successfully achieving your desired results. For that reason, I highly recommend slowing yourself down and taking it easy. There is no rush towards your results, as long as you are making steady and consistent progress. Be patient with yourself.

If you are ready to begin discovering the power of decluttering and are prepared to declutter your life and your house one step at a time, please be sure to enjoy the process along the way!

INTRODUCTION

Congratulations on downloading ***Declutter***!

Over the next six chapters, you are going to be guided on a journey of how you can declutter your life and your home one step at a time. This journey can be a trying one, but it is also highly rewarding and stands to offer you many great benefits along the way. From having a stronger sense of mental clarity and wellbeing to feeling better about your home, there are many benefits that you gain when you focus on decluttering your life.

As you go through this journey, I encourage you to really embrace the act of compassion and understanding. The fact that you have chosen to invest in learning more about the process of decluttering proves that you are serious about making meaningful changes in your life. It also suggests that you may have attempted to do it on your own but found that you were left feeling overwhelmed or at a loss for where to start or what to do. This feeling of frustration and confusion is completely natural, and you are not alone in feeling it. In fact, *most* people feel that way when they begin decluttering their lives and homes! Being compassionate and understanding with yourself and not judging yourself for any feelings that may come up along the way will ensure that you are able to continue along with the process of decluttering.

This book has been designed in a step-by-step process, starting with your mind and leading you to the point of decluttering your social circle and friendships. By following this book in the order it has been presented to you with, you can equip yourself with the necessary resources to successfully achieve each successive step. Attempting to do too much at once or skip over steps could result in an increase in overwhelm and a decreased likelihood of successfully achieving your desired results. For that reason, I highly recommend slowing yourself down and taking it easy. There is no rush towards your results, as long as you are making steady and consistent progress. Be patient with yourself.

If you are ready to begin discovering the power of decluttering and are prepared to declutter your life and your house one step at a time, please be sure to enjoy the process along the way!

Chapter 1: The Power of Decluttering

Have you ever cleaned out your junk drawer and felt that intense burst of energy that made you feel positive, uplifted, and inspired? Maybe it was the console in your car or one of the messier shelves in your pantry, but either way, that moment of seeing that once-cluttered space now clean and organized felt *so good.* Do you remember that feeling? That feeling summarizes the power of decluttering and how it can actually help you live a better life; complete with a greater sense of peace, calm, and efficiency.

The power of decluttering is not only in your mind, either. That positive energy you feel when you declutter a messy space actually supports you in experiencing a greater sense of joy, positivity, and abundance in your life overall. There are many positive benefits to decluttering your life, including the physical and non-physical aspects of it. Before we dive into the 'how,' let's take a moment and explore *why* decluttering has such a powerful impact on your life and what it will actually do for you.

You Will Feel a Greater Sense of Vibrancy

When you declutter your space, your inner world becomes a lot more vibrant and this is reflected in your outer world, too. The more harmony that you experience in your home and in your life, the easier it is for you to be present and live in the moment rather than feeling as though you are constantly being distracted by the disharmonies in your life. As a result of your presence, you will feel a greater sense of radiance and vibrancy in your life, allowing you to show up and enjoy living your life with far greater sincerity and joy than ever before.

Decluttering your life allows you to remove blockages and imbalances from your mind and physical space, clearing up room for you to flow more freely. As a result, your ability to flow into places of happiness and non-resistance become far easier, too. You will feel a fresh sense of inner energy that inspires you to magnetize joy and abundance into your life, which will only further boost your happiness.

While decluttering does not guarantee that you will be laughing and smiling every minute of the day, it does help you anchor in a deeper sense of contentment that is far more sustainable and lasting. So, while you may not feel intense and frequent bursts of positive energy, you will feel a greater sense of true happiness that lingers and keeps you feeling happier about life in general.

Your Schedule Will Clear Up, Big Time

The feelings of overwhelm when your life is cluttered are real, and they have a seriously negative impact on your time. When you have an immense amount of clutter in your life, your schedule always appears to be lacking in extra time for you to be able to actually enjoy your life. You likely find yourself losing minutes or even hours, perhaps, without any clear understanding as to why you have lost them. Maybe you think it is because you are lazy or because you lack personal motivation because that 'extra time' seems to disappear with you hiding out on the couch or filling it in with aimless tasks that do not bring you any joy or fulfillment. In reality, you are likely just experiencing feelings of overwhelm that is preventing you from getting up and actually going about your daily life.

See, in your mind, when you have things you *should* be doing that you don't want to be doing, instead of simply not doing them and doing something more fulfilling or enjoyable, you start wasting time. Somewhere in your mind, you say, "well, if I'm not doing what I *should* be doing, then I shouldn't be doing anything fun, either." This is a way that we attempt to justify why we are not getting things done. Often, the lack of achievement also comes along with excuses like "I'm stressed from work," "I had a headache," or "I deserve a day off." In reality, these excuses are only meant to cover up the reality, which was that you felt overwhelmed by the clutter and you had no idea how to tackle it, so instead, you didn't.

When you tackle clutter effectively and remove it from your life completely, your calendar seems to have so much extra time in it. You are no longer trapped in a cycle of procrastinating from tasks that involve managing your clutter and then doing nothing so that you can justify why nothing got done. Instead, you get it done and you begin to experience an inner sense of openness that gives you permission to go enjoy other things in your life such as reading, hanging out with loved ones, or picking up a new hobby.

You Begin To Move Forward In Life

With all of your spare time, it is inevitable that one of the things that you will accomplish with it is the process of actually moving forward in your life. Now that you have nothing and no one physically or mentally holding you back, you can begin investing in the things that are actually going to draw you forward and help you live a better life. You can invest in things like inner healing, releasing unwanted baggage, finding peace, and taking action towards your lifelong goals. As a result of this action, you are able to clear up your inner life even further and make real progress towards achieving everything you wished that you would achieve in your life.

According to many psychologists, clutter often reflects the unresolved business that you are holding onto in your life. When you begin to move the clutter out, you can bring closure to those things and open up room for you to move forward by taking positive risks in your life. Maybe, releasing your clutter and your attachment to the past allows you to move to a new place, travel more, or pursue your dream job. Maybe, it allows you to release friends that no longer resonate with you, or go ahead and get the dog you have always wanted but never brought home for fear of it destroying your clutter. You can start doing new things and taking new adventures without so much fear of what will happen because you are no longer being held back by your clutter.

You Can Address Your Personal Issues

Another branch of clutter that is keeping you attached to unfinished business is that it can prevent you from experiencing full closure from things that you have experienced in the past. When you dig through your mess and begin getting rid of things, you will find that a lot of objects come forward that bring up old memories and remind you of bad experiences, broken dreams, or moments of grief from your life. When you hold onto things that have these types of negative attachments to them, you essentially bury your feelings and avoid having to actively work through them. Every time you encounter these objects in your house, you may feel a pang of sadness or regret, or maybe even anger. So, holding onto them naturally increases the number of negative experiences that you are having. Finding them may be challenging and may resurface old feelings for you, but getting rid of them once and for all will be incredibly helpful in allowing you to move past your challenges and heal from your personal issues.

As you deep clean each room in your house, as well as your mind, your relationships, your finances, and your life in general, you will find that you begin to experience emotional and mental freedom from things that have been hurting you. This will help you move on from these experiences and have closure surrounding them so that you can fully move forward and embrace the next stages of your life. Even though it may be emotional or challenging in the beginning, it will be fulfilling and helpful in the long run. The closure will support you in moving on for good and welcoming newer experiences into your life that brings you more opportunities to enjoy life and grow from your challenges.

Your Habits Can Be Transformed

Keeping yourself surrounded by the same clutter day in and day out can leave you feeling trapped inside of bad habits that have never effectively served you in living a better life. When you work towards decluttering your house and your life, you begin to experience a change from your standard daily routine. This change is often enough to help jolt you out of any bad habits that you have been feeling entrapped in, while also giving you the room that you need to embrace new positive habits.

Another significant way that decluttering is going to help you eliminate bad habits is through helping you release the triggers that exist for those bad habits to transpire in the first place. For example, say that you have been trying to eat healthier but you find yourself always reaching for sugary treats or snacks in-between meals and it has been preventing you from making positive improvements. Maybe you think that you are weak or incapable of change, so instead, you keep justifying why you are going for the sweets, rather than making a larger change that will prevent you from being able to reinforce negative habits. By decluttering, you can choose to remove the sugars and sweets from your house entirely so that the ability to act on your habits is removed and you have to start making different decisions. When you eliminate the triggers from your life, your bad habits have nothing to thrive on so they naturally diminish and leave you with the opportunity to turn to positive habits, instead.

You Feel More Rested and Less Stressed

Clutter is known for generating high feelings of stress in people who are regularly surrounded by it. Having massive amounts of clutter in your space can leave you feeling higher levels of stress for many different reasons, from feeling obligated to do something about it to feeling stressed out that you cannot find anything or that simple tasks are now harder. There are many ways that clutter can significantly increase the amount of stress that you experience, thus making it significantly harder for you to experience calmness and relaxation.

When you are consistently feeling even small amounts of stress in your life, the continual trigger of negative thoughts and emotions can result in increased levels of cortisol and adrenaline in your body. If these hormones are triggered often enough, they can lead to disturbances in your sleep and in your ability to relax in general. People who are surrounded by a lot of clutter often find themselves struggling to fully rest because they feel a continued sense of stress that lingers with them on a daily basis. By removing the clutter that is causing your stress, you can give yourself the opportunity to enter a deeper state of relaxation and feel more at peace in your life. This increased feeling of general peace allows you to begin feeling a greater sense of ease in your life, as well as an increased ability to experience deep and effective relaxation and sleep. As a result, you no longer begin to carry the effects of prolonged stress around because they are eased by peace.

Chapter 2: Decluttering Your Mindset

The first step to decluttering your life is decluttering your mindset. Your mindset is the part of you that allows you to hold on to clutter in your life, justify why you are doing so, and reinforce negative habits that keep the clutter lingering far past its expiration date. When your mindset is not healthy and focused, it is easy for you to put off doing anything about the clutter in your life because facing it feels uncomfortable or challenging.

Decluttering your mindset gives you the opportunity to understand how decluttering your life will improve your quality of living. It also provides you with the opportunity to empower yourself with the resources that you need to embrace and sustain the practice of decluttering the rest of your life. When you are in the right frame of mind, facing the emotions that may arise when it comes to eliminating unwanted or unhelpful items from your life becomes a lot easier. You will also have an easier time giving yourself permission to eliminate toxic people from your life, make financial changes, and embrace the art of decluttered living in general.

In this chapter, we are going to start by identifying how you can get clear on what matters to you and then declutter your mind so that your mental processes reflect your values. That way, you will have an easier time making more permanent physical changes in your life because you will be mentally equipped with the motivation, energy, and resources to do so. It is important that you start with mindset because without it, you may find yourself failing to actively make any changes in your life or struggling to maintain those changes for a longer period of time. Without your mind on board, reengaging in old habits or letting old triggers pull you back into a cluttered state of living becomes a lot easier.

In order to effectively embrace the practice of changing your mindset, I highly recommend that you pick up a journal that you are going to use to help you address your mindset patterns. In this journal, refrain from having any particular rhyme or reason for how things are organized or what is inside of it. Instead, simply use it to write out your thoughts and get your inner feelings out on paper in any order that they feel like coming out in. That way, you can see exactly what it is that you are holding on to and how it is holding you back. I recommend using this book throughout the entire decluttering process, as it will give you a spot to write down why you are feeling so attached to certain things in your life and how you can release those attachments so that you can embrace a better life.

Identifying Your Core Values

Every single person on the planet has core values, whether they are consciously aware of these values or not. Your core values are things that you care about the most and that you will consistently value above anything else in your life. Your core values highlight what you stand for, what you care about, and why you behave the way that you do. When you are consciously aware of your core values, you can understand what drives you and motivates you and begin living in alignment with them so that you experience a consistent and deep sense of fulfillment. When you are not consciously aware of them, or if you are but you are failing to honor them, your core values become a source of pain because you find yourself living out of alignment with what matters to you. As a result, you begin to enforce bad habits and childish behavior as a way to cope and experience some form of relief from the pain of not honoring your values.

Discovering what your personal values are is imperative because it allows you to begin making conscious changes in your life that will support you in honoring these values. Although your values may seem mysterious and unknown in the present, it is actually not too hard to identify your core values and begin acting in alignment with them, so that you can continue experiencing fulfillment and joy in your life.

Before you begin discovering your core values, it is important that you take a few minutes to discard any values that you may be carrying from society or as a result of the beliefs that others have bestowed upon you. For example, if society tells you that you should value money but you find that money is not that important to you, do not feel obligated to hold financial wealth as one of your core values simply because society said so. Many people, particularly those who do not take the time to discover their core values, hold on to societal values and believe that they genuinely reflect their own personal values, too. If a value does not resonate with you, you are not obligated to maintain that value, even if it seems like you should because society told you that you must.

Once you have given yourself permission to discard the values of the society that do not resonate with you, you can start identifying your core values based on what does matter to you. The best way to do this is to begin journaling about what truly matters to you. If you are not yet sure, consider writing down all of the times when you feel your best in life. The moments that you feel motivated, inspired, and ready to jump into action are typically the same moments that you are living in alignment with your values. Pay attention to what common themes arise in these moments and use them as an opportunity to identify what matters the most to you. These will be your core values.

Overcoming Procrastination

One of the biggest reasons why people procrastinate in their lives is because they are unhappy with the lives that they are living and they use procrastination as a means to avoid doing the things that they don't want to do. While you cannot avoid doing things you do not want to do in certain cases, you can offset this reaction by increasing the number of positive things that you get to enjoy in your daily life. By creating a more harmonious balance between what you enjoy and what you have to get done, it becomes easier to do the things that you need to do because you are approaching your life from a more enjoyable and positive frame of mind.

In addition to balancing out your schedule to accommodate for more of what you enjoy and value, there are also some other ways that you can decrease your tendency to procrastinate and increase your ability to focus and get things done. Many of these practices are rooted in the mind and in learning how to motivate yourself so that you can stop being charmed by distractions are start taking productive actions towards succeeding in achieving your goals.

One great way that you can overcome procrastination is by setting a time restriction on how long you are allowed to put things off for and then actually adhering to that restriction. For example, say you have a tendency to get distracted anytime you are engaging in an activity that needs to get done. You might set a rule for yourself that you will give yourself the opportunity to spend 5 minutes being distracted before you get started, and then set a timer and fulfill those 5 minutes with distractions. This is an opportunity to get anything distracting out of the way so that you can clearly focus once you get to work. Then, if you notice that you tend to get distracted again at certain points into your work, you can schedule additional distraction breaks. For example, say around one hour into doing any task, you find yourself feeling distracted and struggling to stay focused. Rather than trying to push through the distraction and work with half of your focus, you can instead give yourself 5 minutes to be distracted and then return to focusing on your task at hand. By intentionally giving yourself permission to take 5 minutes here and there to indulge in your distractions, you ensure that you are not allowing them to take over and prevent you from getting started or completing your work.

Another thing that you can do is promise yourself a reward anytime you engage in a new task and fully completes it. Rewards show you that it is worthwhile to do things, even if they are things that you do not necessarily enjoy so that you can begin getting tasks done without such a struggle. Plus, they are a fun way to celebrate your success and your devotion to achieving your goals.

The final tip I want to give you is a mindset strategy that you can use called rephrasing. Rephrasing requires you to assess your inner dialogue around the subject and then consider how you can adjust it to keep yourself motivated and ready to achieve your tasks at hand. Often, when you are procrastinating, the inner dialogue that you are engaging in surrounding the task at hand is negative towards the task that needs to be achieved. By adjusting what you are saying to yourself, it becomes easier for you to find the energy and motivation to get up and get the task done. For example, instead of saying "I hate doing dishes. I don't want to do them. I'll do them later," you might say, "I love having a clean kitchen. I'm going to get it done so I can enjoy my clean space."

Releasing Negative Thought Patterns

Negative thought patterns are a form of mental clutter that does not serve you in any way, shape, or form. When you engage in negative thought patterns, you pressure yourself into feeling unconfident, incapable, or overwhelmed. Negative thought patterns are often at the foundation of every bad habit or experience we keep ourselves engaged in because we are able to justify them by lessening ourselves through our inner dialogue. Not only will they result in you lacking confidence and self-esteem, but they will also result in you feeling as though there is nothing positive or worthwhile for you to look forward to in your life. People who are constantly feeding into pessimistic thought patterns often find themselves feeling negative about everything that is going on in their lives. If you are someone who regularly complains, sees the bad in people or situations, or feels like there is nothing positive about yourself or the world around you, chances are that you are engaging in negative thought patterns.

A great way to begin decluttering your mind by releasing negative thought patterns is by engaging in activities such as cognitive behavioral therapy. This form of therapy does not require you to actually go and see a therapist so that you can check in on your negative thinking patterns. Instead, it allows you to identify what negative thoughts are leading to the negative emotions that you are experiencing and how you can intercept these thoughts so that you can adjust your emotions and, in turn, feel more confident and motivated.

In order to begin enforcing cognitive behavioral therapy in your own life, you can start keeping a journal where you track your thoughts and coinciding feelings on a regular basis. Each time you notice an intense or obvious negative emotion coming into your life, stop and consider what thoughts you are having and how they are contributing to that negative emotion. Then, once you have a general idea of what negative thought patterns you tend to follow, start consciously choosing new inner dialogues and activities to help you overcome these negative thoughts.

Increasing Your Mental Resiliency

Many people who are experiencing intense clutter in their lives and in their minds are also struggling with mental resiliency. Mental resiliency is the tool that you can use to help you focus your mind and bounce back from challenging or emotional situations with greater ease. You can build mental resiliency through practices like meditation, mindfulness, and rest. You can also build it by finding purpose in your life, as having a purpose is known to help people feel a greater sense of urgency when it comes to moving forward in their lives. People who lack purpose often find themselves feeling like there is no point in moving forward or accomplishing challenging tasks because there is no purpose behind the action itself. When you discover what your purpose is or create purpose and meaning in your day-to-day life, even as simple as cultivating your own contentment, you give yourself a reason to stay dedicated to more challenging practices.

You can also build your mental resiliency by choosing to put things into perspective and through realizing that not everything is as challenging as it may sound. When you see that all of your problems can be overcome and that they will not last forever, it becomes easier to prevent them from feeling all-consuming. This means that you no longer feel as though you simply cannot overcome challenges because they do not seem quite so large and daunting. When it comes to decluttering your mind, having resiliency is imperative as this is the key that is going to help you bounce back even after you have setbacks. Any time you find yourself struggling to maintain your clean space or feeling as though there is no reason for you to get up and make changes in your life, you can fall back on your mental resiliency as a tool to help you move forward and achieve success.

If you're enjoying this audiobook, I would love if you went to audible and just left a short review.

Chapter 3: Decluttering Your Home

The next step in decluttering your life is decluttering your home. They say that having a messy home reflects the fact that you likely also have a messy frame of mind, meaning that you likely hold onto a lot of stress and overwhelm. Now that you have made the conscious effort of moving past the mental clutter, you need to begin working on cleaning up your home, so that it can support you in having less stress to worry about. When you live in a clean and comfortable space, it becomes easier for you to rest, concentrate, and focus on achieving what you desire in your life because you are not wasting your attention on frustrations that arise in the midst of clutter.

In this chapter, we are going to look into how you can declutter your home and rejuvenate your living space. You are going to discover how you can eliminate clutter and create a cozier environment so that your home nurtures your ability to rest and relax, while also providing you a great launch pad for setting out to achieve all of your goals. You will never realize just how valuable your home is in regards to your mental wellness and your ability to live a successful life until you declutter it and let go of every block that has been holding you back.

How to Tackle the Decluttering of your Home

When you are decluttering your home, it is important that you do it on a step-by-step basis. If you are reading this book, the chances are that your home feels pretty overwhelming and frustrating to you right now. You may have already tried to declutter but it proved to be ineffective or you got overwhelmed and annoyed and were unable to finish the task. By working towards decluttering your home one step at a time, you can ensure that you are ready to face each task. You also prevent it from feeling daunting and overwhelming so it becomes easier for you to actually stay devoted to the task and get the job done.

I suggest following this chapter step-by-step in order so that you are able to accomplish the decluttering process in a way that will work alongside improving your inner contentment and wellbeing. By starting with the bedroom, you ensure that you are in a cozy and comfortable space each night when you go to sleep. Then, you can begin tackling each room based on how frequently they are used and how much they affect your sense of wellbeing.

Decluttering Your Bedroom

Your bedroom is where you lay your head to rest at night unless it is overwhelming and uncomfortable. Having a bedroom that is filled with clutter or that continually looks messy can be extremely stressful and overwhelming. Laying your head to sleep in a room that is cluttered can result in you not getting a sound sleep, or in you struggling to get any sleep at all. By tackling your bedroom first, you can ensure that you are able to start getting a sound sleep and improving your mental well-being right away using the art of decluttering as your secret weapon.

Below are six steps that you can use to declutter your room right now:

Eliminate Unwanted Clothes

Clothes tend to formulate the bulk of most messes in bedrooms. The best way for you to overcome this is to donate unwanted clothes so that you are not shoveling them out of the way every time you look for clothes that you actually want to wear.

Use Your Hamper

Instead of throwing your worn clothes on the floor, toss them into a hamper so that they are contained and cleaner looking. This also prevents you from having to determine what is clean and what isn't. Make sure that you get into the habit of putting clothes directly into your hamper so that you don't have to do it later.

Use Containers to Contain the Clutter

If you tend to store little things in your room such as jewelry, keys, or other little things, start using small containers to contain them. Bowls, trays, and small baskets or boxes are great tools for organizing smaller clutter that does not have a space to stay long-term.

Organize Your Closet

Your closet is an important area of your room to organize, too. Invest in shelves, shoe storage, and proper hangers and start making use of the space that you have in your closet. Get into the habit of hanging your clothes and returning your shoes to their spot so that they are always organized and out of the way.

Use Minimalistic Decorations

Make sure that the decorations you use in your bedroom are minimalistic and calm and relaxed in their design. Having anything too bold, bright, or overwhelming can keep your mind busy and prevent you from having a sound sleep each night. Think in terms of decorating with minimalistic paintings, candles, and soft fabrics.

Decluttering Your Kitchen

Your kitchen should be your next order of business. You use your kitchen on a daily basis, which means that it can quickly and easily become cluttered and messy consistently. In fact, you may feel like all you ever do is clean your kitchen when you are home because of the number of dishes, cookware, and utensils that you go through. Organizing your kitchen and decluttering it will help you eliminate this stress and keep your kitchen cleaner so that you do not feel like you are constantly battling a messy space.

Below are seven steps you can take to create a cleaner kitchen.

Eliminate the Excess Junk

Start by getting rid of all of the dishes, small appliances, and other odds and ends that you don't use anymore. Kitchen cabinets and drawers tend to be a place where junk goes to hide, so pulling everything out and eliminating unwanted space is a good place to start.

Take Advantage of Storage Space

As you begin putting your kitchen back together, be sure to take advantage of storage space when you are putting everything back. Do not be afraid to hang hooks so that you can make use of vertical storage, or add lazy Susan's into your cupboards for easier access.

Keep Your Counters Clear

Counters tend to accumulate a lot of mess and look disastrous on a consistent basis. Eliminate everything from your counters except for your coffee pot and your microwave. Make a rule that nothing gets stored on the counters anymore.

Use Storage Solutions for Cleaner Drawers and Cupboards

There are many incredible tools that you can buy to organize your drawers and cupboards. Get a matching storage set for all of your dry ingredients, a functional utensil tray for your utensils, and small baskets to organize other odds and ends into.

Build a Communications Center

One thing that tends to build up in the kitchen is the day-to-day tools like purses, keys, cell phone chargers, and other odds and ends. Creating a communications center to store all of these things makes it much easier for you to avoid having them scattered about on the counter. Outfit your space with a calendar, some hanging hooks, and a small drawer set if you can so that you have plenty of space to store things and keep them off of your counters.

Clean Out Underneath Your Sink

Whether you store cleaners, garbage, or both underneath your sink, this space can accumulate a lot of junk if you are not careful. Pull everything out, wipe it down, and only replace the things that you actually use or need. Toss the rest.

Clean Out Your Food Supply

The final thing you need to do when decluttering your kitchen is to clean out your food supply. Eliminate all of the food from your pantry, cupboards, fridge, and freezer that you are not eating. Even if it has not yet expired, do not keep it if you do not want it. It only takes up space and makes you feel guilty that you wasted your money on it.

Decluttering Your Living Room

The next space you need to declutter is your living room. The living room tends to be another area that accumulates a lot of day-to-day essentials and random clutter since it tends to be where most people spend their time when they are home, aside from the kitchen. Decluttering your living room requires you to ensure that you are staying consistent when it comes to keeping everything out of the living room long-term.

Below are four strategies that you can use to declutter your living room.

Return Everything to Where It Belongs

Begin by taking a moment to remove everything out of the living room that does not belong there. Return clothes back to where they belong, put their shoes in their space, bring dishes back into the kitchen, and put the toys back in your kids' rooms.

Use A Declutter Basket

Decluttering baskets are great in living rooms because they make returning stuff to other parts of the house easier. Keep a basket in your living room and each time you find something in the living room that doesn't belong, toss it in the basket. At the end of each day, put everything back where it belongs.

Organize Your Media Cabinet

Media cabinets can become messy with cords, games, movies, and other gadgets. Take some time to organize your media cabinet by organizing your cords, stacking games and DVDs nicely, and putting other odds and ends into small storage containers that you can store in the media cabinet. That way, everything looks neat and it is also easier to find.

Minimize Your Decorations

While your living room offers far more flexibility when it comes to decorations, you should still be cautious about what you add to this space. Think about decorating with quality, not quantity, so that you do not have so many things to dust, move around, or organize when it comes time to clean up.

Decluttering Your Bathrooms

While your bathrooms are used multiple times a day, they are not necessarily known for being the worst when it comes to clutter. However, because the type of clutter that accumulates is often filled with various liquids and products, they can spill over and create an unsightly mess. For that reason, you need to have a proper decluttering regimen in place that minimizes the amount of stuff you keep and keeps it organized so that you are not finding your bathroom looking overwhelmed with a mess.

Below are three strategies that you can use to declutter your bathroom.

Eliminated Unwanted Products

Products that are typically stored in the bathroom can be expensive, which is why most people feel guilty about throwing away the things that they are not using. However, this can result in you having a tremendous amount of clutter built up in a small space. Start your decluttering process by throwing away every single product that you have not used in more than one month.

Clean Absolutely Everything Off

Now that you have eliminated unwanted products, you need to clean everything off. Wipe dirt and grime off of product bottles, wipe out cupboards and drawers, and wipe down your sink and mirror while you are at it. Then, put everything away neatly in the newly cleaned space.

Use Effective Storage Solutions

When it comes to putting things back, make sure that you are doing so in a way that makes sense. Consider investing in small baskets to organize products into, use a shower caddy to store your shower products in, and get a toilet roll holder to hold extra toilet paper rolls in the bathroom. You may also consider using a small shelf under your sink so that you have more storage space for products and beauty tools.

Decluttering Storage

There are likely many other storage areas in your home that have not yet been discussed in this chapter. While these are not used as frequently or intensely as other areas in your home, they can become extremely messy and overwhelming if you are not careful. Coat closets, storage closets, garages, storage rooms, and other spaces can become messy if you are not maintaining them well.

Below are three strategies that you can use to declutter your storage spaces.

Commit To Going through Everything

It may be an overwhelming task, but you should commit to going through everything that you have in storage. If you have not done this in a while, you may be surprised to find that you are holding onto a lot of junk that you do not need anymore. Set aside a day, or a few days, where you are going to go through your storage spaces and organize everything. In that time, eliminate everything you do not want, pull out things you want to start using regularly, and organize the things that you want to put back into storage into logical categories.

Use Labeled Bins

When you have determined what is ready to go back into storage, you can go ahead and purchase some labeled bins to store everything in. Even if you already have some bins, you might consider purchasing all new ones that are similar in size, shape, and color. That way, when everything is put away, it looks visually appealing, which will help it produce less stress each time you look at it. Label bins clearly so that you know exactly what has been stored inside of them.

Keep the Space Clean

Even though it may seem pointless, commit to regularly vacuuming and dusting your storage spaces. Doing so will ensure that you are not accumulating large amounts of dust and dirt in these areas, which will help them look and feel more organized each time you go into them.

Chapter 4: Decluttering Your Finances

The next task you are going to want to tackle when it comes to decluttering your life is decluttering your finances. Finances tend to become overwhelmed with excess burdens, money leaking out in places that it shouldn't be, and chaos or confusion being thrown into the pile. If you have no idea where your money is going, find yourself paying for bills that you don't even recognize, or have services that are going unused, it is time for you to do a financial decluttering. That way, you can ensure that you are not wasting your money, that you have more to save, and that when you spend it, you actually spend it on things that are meaningful and purposeful.

In this chapter, we are going to explore four critical areas that you need to consider in your finances when it comes to building budgets. These areas are going to support you in making sure that your finances are being properly managed. In doing so, not only will you bring less chaos and confusion around your finances, but you will also bring more peace and relaxation into your life. Finances tend to be one of the biggest areas where chaos and overwhelming stresses seep into people's lives, especially if they find themselves coming under financial strain on a regular basis. Organizing your finances will ensure that you are not wasting money or stressing unnecessarily over things that do not matter.

Mastering the Art of Budgeting

Budgeting is a valuable tool that can help ensure that you are not wasting finances on unnecessary expenses or overspending in areas of your life where you should be saving more. Creating a functional budget for you is extremely simple.All it requires of you is for you to take an honest account of what you are earning and what you are spending on a monthly basis. This way, you can identify where your money needs to be spent and how you can be spending it wisely on a weekly and monthly basis.

The best way to start your budget is to write down how much money you bring in each month. Write this down on a piece of paper at the top of the page. Then, underneath that number, write down every mandatory expense that you need to be spending on a monthly basis. This includes your car payments, gas bills, rent, utilities, groceries, and other mandatory expenses that you need to be paying in order to maintain your basic needs. Underneath those, include the additional expenses that you tend to find yourself using on a consistent basis. This typically includes money spent on clothes, entertainment, and other more frivolous purchases that you may enjoy making on a monthly basis. This is going to give you an idea of where your money is being spent and how so that you have a clearer understanding as to how your money is being used.

As you go through your budget, take account of any subscriptions or other monthly expenses that you are incurring that are not necessary or that you do not actually use. For example, if you have a Netflix subscription or some magazine subscriptions but you find that you are never actively using them, you can cancel these and save yourself the monthly expense. That way, you are not wasting money on things that do not matter to you.

The last thing that you need to do is consider how much you want to be saving on a monthly basis. The best way to do this is to create savings goals for you. You should have short-term savings goals that you want to see met in the next 6-12 months, as well as long-term savings goals that you have for five, ten, fifteen, and twenty years from now. If you are significantly younger and you have many more years to go before you reach a retirement age, set your retirement savings goal as well. With these goals in mind, calculate how much you need to be saving on a monthly basis in order to meet these goals. Then, go ahead and factor that in as a necessary expense on your monthly bills. This savings value should come before any of your luxury expenses such as entertainment, as this money will be used to help you sustain a higher quality of living in the long run.

Releasing Financial Burdens You Don't Need

It is important that you really crack down on financial burdens that you are incurring that you do not need. Financial burdens can be anything from subscriptions that you are not using to debt that you are not paying off quick enough. Getting clear on what funds are being wasted on expenses such as this will help you determine whether or not your budget is working in your favor. Eliminating unnecessary expenses and debt will ensure that you are not spending money that you do not need to be spending on a monthly basis.

If you are attempting to cut down on your debt, I recommend putting this above anything else for a while. Get strict on the amount of money that you are willing to spend on new purchases until your debt is completely cleared so that you are no longer wasting money on unnecessary expenses such as high-interest fees and annual charges. That way, your debt is cleared faster and you actually end up saving significantly more every single month.

Some people accumulate a high amount of debt which can make looking at your debt and getting serious on how much you owe scary or even nauseating. Debt can be uncomfortable and frustrating if you are not taking control over it, which makes it understandable as to why so many people attempt to avoid the reality of their debt. Even so, if you want to have a cleaner financial life, you need to eliminate unnecessary debt from your life. The best way to do this is to write down exactly how much you owe and create a plan for how you are going to pay it off. Then, pay into that debt every single month until it is completely eliminated. Avoid spending money, in any way, that could further increase your debt until you have completely paid it off and you are confident that you can manage your debt more wisely in the future.

Having Weekly Spending Limits

Most people want to enjoy the money that they earn so they find themselves regularly indulging in spending money on things like coffees, clothes, convenience services, and other unnecessary expenses. When it is not managed effectively, these types of expenses can quickly rack up and result in you having no money left. In order to avoid spending every last dollar you have on unnecessary expenses, start setting weekly spending limits for yourself. Give yourself a fixed amount that you are allowed to spend on enjoyable things on a weekly basis and be strict in adhering to that amount. That way, you are no longer spending money faster than you are making it and committing to things like paying off debt and saving funds becomes a lot easier for you.

Your weekly spending limit should be reasonable, and it should always come last after your necessary expenses, your debt repayment, and your savings funds. Choose a limit that is going to give you a bit of cash to have fun with, without taking away from other expenses that are more important. Once you pay off your debt or begin earning a higher income, you can increase the number of funds that you have to spend on a weekly basis. Until then, be strict with yourself and your money and commit to paying off your debt now, so that you can pay for your fun and entertainment with ease and less stress later.

Taking the Occasional Cash Freeze Break

If you are someone who tends to spend money without thinking about it, or who relies on things like retail therapy to help you get through challenging times, it is time for you to engage in what is known as a "cash freeze breaks." These breaks are things that some people engage in from time to time to encourage themselves to find other ways to deal with a bad mood or boredom. The rules are simple: for a fixed amount of time, usually a week, you will not spend any money unless it is going towards mandatory bills and expenses. No spending money on entertainment, additional food items, or anything else that would be considered not absolutely necessary in the way of having your basic needs met.

Doing spending freezes allows you to become creative in finding other ways to deal with the emotions or feelings that typically lead to you spending money unnecessarily. Not only does this encourage you to choose healthier coping methods, but it also prevents you from cluttering your house up with unnecessary impulse buys again. That way, you are not bringing home things that will only be donated or thrown out at a later date. Engaging in a spending freeze any time you find your impulsive purchases becoming excessive will ensure that you are staying on top of your spending habits and maintaining a healthy, clutter-free relationship with your finances.

Chapter 5: Decluttering Your Relationships

Relationships have the ability to become toxic and overwhelming in your life. If you are engaging in relationships that do not bring you joy, make you feel inspired or enriched, or help you to live a better life, chances are that you are carrying clutter in your relationships. As adults, we tend to not have much time to allot to things like friends and hobbies because we have so many demands on our time, such as work, family, and other errands that need to be run in order to maintain our daily lives. For that reason, it is imperative that you stay strict on who enters your life and how they contribute to the quality of your life. Cluttering up what little time you have to invest in friends and fun with people who are leaving you feeling frustrated, uncomfortable, or pained are only going to result in you feeling an increase in stress and overwhelm. As a result, you are going to experience a lower quality of life and a reduced desire to contribute to your experiencing more joy and positivity.

In this chapter, we are going to look at ways that you can identify clutter in your social circle and eliminate the people who are not contributing to the wellbeing of your general life. By identifying toxic people or meaningless relationships and eliminating them, you give yourself more time to devote to the relationships that actually mean something to you in your life. That way, you are spending what time you do have on relationships that are enriching and that lift you up and help you feel inspired to continue doing better in your everyday life.

Identifying Clutter in Your Social Circle

The first thing that you need to do when it comes to decluttering your social circle is to identify where the clutter actually exists. They say that you are the sum of the five people that you spend most of your time with. Looking at the five people that you spend your time with helps you to determine who they are and, as a result, who you are. If these people are inspiring, uplifting, positive, and motivated, then chances are you are surrounding yourself with great people who are helping lift you up and motivate you in your own life. However, if you look around and see people who lack motivation, who regularly make excuses for themselves, and who struggle to make positive changes in their lives, then chances are that you are struggling with all of the same things. For that reason, you need to get clear on where the clutter lies and how you can clean it up to avoid being dragged down anymore.

In some relationships, the clutter is not necessarily the person themselves, but instead, in the way that your relationship manifests. For example, maybe you have a relationship with a really positive and inspiring person but the only time you spend together is spent doing meaningless tasks or things that you do not enjoy.

In that case, the relationship may be cluttered with you not being willing to speak up for yourself or what you enjoy, or with the fact that even though you are both great people, you simply do not connect in an effective manner.

Identifying clutter in your relationships and in your social circle, in general, helps you begin making effective action plans so that you can determine what needs to be done, allowing you to experience less clutter in your relationships. Whether that is adjusting how you spend your time together, speaking up for yourself more and building more of a quality connection, or moving on and finding a friend who is better suited for you, that will ultimately be up to you.

Some people are unwilling to leave everyone behind, particularly if the relationship in question is one that is shared between someone you care about but do not necessarily get along with very well, such as a parent or a sibling. In some cases, this may even be a lifelong best friend whom you do not want to cut out of your life but whom you struggle to experience positive interactions with anymore. In these scenarios, there are many different solutions that you can come up with to avoid having to actually remove said person from your life. For example, spending less time with them, or being more selective about what you engage in together so that there is less of an opportunity for the negative or toxic traits to arise. You may also consider chatting with this person and encouraging them to engage in some healthy self-reflection so that they can see where their own negativity may be bringing them down. If you do choose to engage in a conversation like this, make sure that you do it gently and mindfully, so that it doesn't sound like you are attacking or belittling the other person. That way, it is more likely to be a constructive conversation than one that results in them feeling angry and an argument transpiring in your relationship, which can lead to further stress.

Removing Toxic Relationships from Your Life

When it comes to dealing with toxic relationships in your life, finding the right way to navigate the ending of these relationships can be challenging. You may struggle to understand how you can approach the situation in a way that is going to allow you to confidently and successfully end the relationship without causing too many hurt feelings. Unfortunately, hurt feelings are almost completely unavoidable when it comes to navigating the ending of challenging relationships in your life, so ending the relationship in a way where absolutely no feelings are hurt is going to be tough. For that reason, it is important that you understand that hurt feelings are going to be a part of the equation so that you can manage it in a way that minimizes the number of feelings that are being hurt.

With that in mind, there are a few things that you can do to end toxic relationships in a healthy and positive manner so that you can avoid doing extra or unnecessary damage in the process. The following three steps will help you successfully end unhealthy and toxic relationships in the most effective and polite manner possible.

Be Completely Honest From the Start

If you have already tried using other methods to improve the relationship that you share with a toxic person and they do not seem to be working for you, then it is time for you to move on to a new plan. That plan should be for you to completely end the relationship so that you can avoid having to suffer from the other person's toxic behaviors and attitude any longer. In order for you to successfully end a toxic relationship, you need to be completely honest right from the start. Being honest will prevent you from creating further hurt feelings by lying or trying to protect their feelings, which are already being hurt because you are ending your relationship with them. The best way to lessen the blow is to be honest and kind with everything you say.

Avoid Playing the Blame Game

When you end a relationship that is toxic, avoid playing the blame game and making it sound like you are attacking the other person or victimizing yourself from the relationship. Even though they have been toxic, recognize that there is a chance that you have been contributing to the toxic behavior in some way. In realizing this, avoid bringing up any arguments that may make it sound like you are ending the relationship because the other person is in any way bad. Even if they have done bad things, do not blame them or become harsh or attacking towards them in pointing out the truth. Always be polite and use "I" statements so that you own your feelings and your responsibility in the situation. That way, you are not hurting their feelings and you are not creating the opportunity for them to victimize themselves and potentially use that against you in the future.

End the Relationship Completely

If you have arrived at the point where you feel as though you need to end a relationship with someone, make sure that you completely end the relationship that you share with this person. Trying to hold onto the relationship or create hope when there is no hope to be had will only result in you feeling prolonged effects of their toxic behaviors. Cut off the relationship completely by eliminating all means of communication and contact with this person. Do not call them or text them any longer, do not keep them on your social media accounts, and do not spend time with them if you come across them in public. Instead, nod or say a polite hello and move along. Attempting to rekindle toxic relationships is only going to result in you exposing yourself to the toxic behavior once again. As hard as it is, you need to completely end the relationship and keep it that way so that you are not bringing the clutter of toxicity back into your life over and over again.

Cleaning Up Your Social Media

Another part of your social life that you need to focus on cleaning up is your social media. Social media has a tendency to be a place where you accumulate a lot of friends and followers who hang around and rarely interact with you or maintain a relationship with you. Frequently, these relationships are held onto out of obligation or for no real reason at all, such as when you add people you went to high school with and then never saw – or talked to – again. Although it may seem nice and comforting to have these people around, the reality is that you are just holding onto clutter for no real reason. Instead of holding onto friends and followers on Facebook, Instagram, Pinterest, and other accounts that you spend time on, regularly purge your friends' lists and eliminate anyone whom you do not genuinely enjoy interacting with.

You should also set aside time to do this with your email. Our inboxes can quickly become flooded with so many different newsletters, spam messages, and other strange messages that come in from seemingly nowhere. These messages can be overwhelming and can waste your time, as you have to go through and delete them every single time that they come in. Instead of accumulating junk mail in your inbox, spend time unsubscribing from every email list that you do not actually care about receiving. Furthermore, avoid signing up for newsletters in the future unless you actually stand to gain something meaningful or valuable out of them. That way, you do not have to waste your time continually purging your email account over and over again.

Lastly, go on your phone and sort through all of your contacts and text messages. Go ahead and eliminate any contacts that you no longer require or use, and erase any text messages that are not important. Though this may seem unnecessary or pointless to you, it can actually do a world of wonders on your mindset. Not having to scroll past the names of people you no longer talk to means no longer having an uncomfortable feeling of being obligated to reach out to them and see how they are doing, despite it being totally unnecessary and even pointless. Instead, simply eliminate these people from your contact list, so that you do not have to worry about them any longer.

Being More Present atthe Moment

Now that you have eliminated everything that has been creating stress and overwhelming feelings in your life in regards to your relationships and social circle, you can start focusing on taking advantage of your new clutter-free space! Spend time focusing on learning how to become present at the moment so that you can stay present and genuinely enjoy the time that you share with the people who matter to you. By staying present and enjoying each moment for what it is, you maximize the quality of your friendships and they become even more rewarding and enjoyable. As a result, you are able to feel more enriched by your relationships and make sure that *you* aren't the one bringing clutter into the relationship and making it toxic.

Being present is an opportunity for you to unite your uncluttered mindset with your uncluttered relationships and experience more joy and positivity in your life. As you begin to embrace presence in your relationships, seek to begin working on new ways to enjoy these relationships even further. Take up hobbies with your friends, enjoy trying new things, fully engage in the experiences that you share, and make each moment meaningful. When you share time together, put your phone down, and avoid stressing or worrying about things that truly do not matter. Do not engage in gossip, complain about everything under the sun, and bring an overall negative energy to the relationship. Instead, work towards creating a positive, enjoyable, and real relationship with the people that you care about.

If presence is particularly challenging for you because your mind still tends to be overwhelmed by clutter, start using some presence practices to help you bring your focus back into the moment. You can do this by using your negative thought pattern reprogramming practices from chapter 2 actively during the time you share with friends, engaging in self-awareness, and practicing self-reflection. By truly paying attention to how you spend your time and where you place your focus, you can ensure that you are only spending your time on things that matter in your life.

Making Time for the Ones You Love

The last thing you need to do when it comes to decluttering your relationships is decluttering the excuses that prevent you from not investing more time and energy into your relationships. Now that your house is clean, your finances are cleared, and you are no longer being overwhelmed by negative thoughts, you can start enjoying more time with the people you love. You can do this by making sure that you actually set aside time for you to spend with your loved ones so that you are seeing them and investing in your relationship with them on a regular basis.

The best way to make sure that you are consistently setting aside time for your loved ones is to schedule aside a bit of time each week to invest in your relationships. You can spend this time physically visiting with them, or talking with them on the phone if visiting is not an option. You can also ensure that every now and again, you send them a text message or an email letting them know that you are thinking about them and taking a moment to catch up with them and see how they are doing. By regularly investing your time and energy into your meaningful relationships, you ensure that you are keeping your relationships fulfilled and that they thrive. Through actions like this, your loved ones know that you care about them and feel as though they are genuinely meaningful to you. As a result, your relationships grow even stronger and the rewards that you reap from them are increased as you derive even more joy and meaning from your relationships.

If you're enjoying this book, I would appreciate it if you went to the place of purchase and left a short positive review. Thank you

Chapter 6: Healthy Habits for Decluttering

You have now successfully invested in decluttering all of the most important aspects of your life. From your mindset to your home, you have discovered everything you need to know in order to fully declutter your life and start experiencing greater joy and rewards from it. Of course, there are always ways for you to improve your ability to declutter and stay clutter-free and stress-free, so in this chapter, I am going to show you how you can engage in healthy habits for decluttering your life even further. You should implement these habits into your life to ensure that you are experiencing the most fulfillment and joy that you possibly can from your life.

Take Things Slowly, There Is No Rush

When it comes to accomplishing something like decluttering your life, most of us have a tendency to get a massive wave of motivation that results in us wanting to get everything done all at once. While this motivation can be powerful, it can also be overwhelming and can lead to you struggling to get anything done. Instead of trying to get it all done at once, give yourself permission to take your time and work through the decluttering process at a rate that is more reasonable for you. This does not mean that you should infuse the process with more procrastination, but don't be afraid to span your decluttering out over a few weeks or a month so that you have plenty of time to get everything done without enduring quite so much stress.

One of the biggest reasons why people become so overwhelmed by decluttering is that they are trying to get everything done immediately. You need to realize that it has taken you a long time to accumulate all of the clutter that you currently have, so it will also take you some time to eliminate it. Although the elimination process will be quicker because it is more intentional and focused, it will still take time. Give yourself the time you need to successfully get through all of the tasks so that you do not experience so much overwhelm and stress along the way.

Be Practical about What You Can Achieve

When it comes to eliminating clutter from your life, you also need to be practical. If you are someone who has been known for hoarding a lot more than you need, then completely eliminating everything the first time around may be excessive and extremely overwhelming for you to embrace. You may need to take things slowly and declutter in phases, by eliminating a few things at a time until you reach a state that feels more comfortable to you. That way, you are not shocking yourself by getting rid of everything and feeling a sense of fear and discomfort as you attempt to get used to not having any of your previous comforts around.

This is especially true when it comes to dealing with finances. When you work towards decluttering your finances, you may find yourself becoming intensely strict on your budget and attempting to cut down on absolutely everything. While this is not harmful in most cases, in some cases, it can become overwhelming or overly restricting if you find yourself trying to achieve too much at once. Instead of trying to get everything done in one go, be practical about what you can accomplish and build from there.

Do Not Be Afraid To Ask For Support

When you are decluttering, it is not unreasonable to ask people to support you and help you successfully get through the process of decluttering. This is even more important if you are someone who struggles with mobility issues or who has some form of physical limitation that prevents you from being able to do too much at once. Instead of attempting to pressure yourself into doing everything alone, be willing to ask for the support of those around you. See who is willing to help you and then do not be afraid to call on them when you need it.

Friends and family can be supportive by helping you pack boxes, organize your belongings back into your new containers, or transport unwanted goods to donation drop-offs. If they are willing to, asking them to help you can be a powerful way to get through everything without feeling quite as stressed out. When you ask, make sure that you truly give yourself permission to receive their help along the way. If you are feeling ashamed about your space or about the mess that you have accumulated, realize that your friends and family have likely already seen it or are experiencing similar issues in their own lives. Most people are not afraid of clutter, nor will they think any less of you if they see that you have clutter in your home. If they do, they are likely individuals that fall into the "toxic" or "clutter" category in your relationships, so letting go of them is not unreasonable.

Take Before and After Photographs

A great way to motivate yourself to keep going and to celebrate how far you have come is to take before and after photographs of your space (to positively inspire you by) as so positive and inspired by the work that you have done, so that it will feel easier for you to move through the cleaning process. Snapping before photographs of rooms, drawers, and messy corners and then snapping after pictures is a great way for you to really see how much work you have done and how much better it looks. When you look at these pictures, you will feel to understand the meaning behind it all and celebrate yourself for your success.

You can also use these photographs to motivate you anytime you see your house becoming messy or cluttered again. Simply sneaking a peek at your before picture and remembering how much work it took for you to get from there to your newer clutter-free space may be plenty to help encourage you to stay on track with your wiser spending habits, your cleaning habits, and your intentional decluttering habits.

Be Compassionate With Yourself

Many people find that decluttering can be incredibility emotional, and they are rarely ready to endure the emotions that come with decluttering. When you eliminate clutter from your house, you may feel all sorts of different feelings. From embarrassment and shame around how far you have let it get to, to feelings of anger and resentment for the memories that are being triggered by your clutter, you may experience many emotions along the way. Being patient and compassionate with yourself when you are decluttering is essentialso that you do not add any additional unnecessary stress to the mix by belittling or bullying yourself in the process.

Realize that your accumulation of clutter was not intentional, nor was it ever meant to cause stress or frustration in your current life. It is likely that you accumulated this clutter by accident, or as a way to cope with challenging emotions that you were not ready to face in the past. If you find that the experience becomes too emotional, use this as an opportunity to lean on your support system, or even begin talking to a therapist for a while. To have someone to talk to about the emotions that are being brought up, especially if they are relating to grief or anger, can be a great way to work through unresolved issues that you may have been holding onto alongside your clutter. Doing this will ensure that you are staying healthy and mentally supported along the way so that you are not feeling so burdened by everything that you are facing.

Make It a Fun Experience

Just because you are cleaning does not mean that you cannot have fun! If you find decluttering to be boring and laborious, consider including activities to make it a more fun experience. Turn on some music and dance along to it, or see how much you can get done during a single song. Give yourself rewards along the way, spend time playing with the gadgets that you have uncovered and seeing if they will have any purpose in your life, and genuinely find joy in the process. You might even make it a game to see how much you can donate. Maybe, if the donation process is more challenging for you, you might consider making up pretend scenarios in your head of the future people who are going to use your items and get joy from them. This will help it not only become more of a game but will also help you see the benefit and value behind what you are doing. The more fun you make it; the easier it will be for you to continue on with the process.

Use a Quarantine Practice If You Need To

If you are attempting to decide what you want to get rid of but you are unsure about whether or not you are ready to get rid of some things, consider using the quarantine method to help you officially make up your mind. This is going to support you in deciding what you truly do want to get rid of, and what you may prefer to keep instead. The quarantine method essentially requires you to have a box or two where you will place items that you are unsure about. Everything you are questioning will go into this box and then be left for a month, maybe two at the very most. Anything that does not get retrieved from the box in that time should be donated so that you are not holding onto anything that you are not going to use.

The quarantine method is not only great for helping you eliminate unwanted things, but also for helping you avoid purchasing new things that you may not actually need or even want. In order to use it to help you shop more wisely, simply consider what landed in the box last time and how you had believed it would be more valuable to you than it was. Then, consider if what you are looking to purchase will actually be valuable to you or if you are going to end up putting it in the quarantine box or donation bin in the near future. If you find that it is likely going to end up there, you can simply save yourself the expense and avoid wasting your money by not purchasing the item at all. That way, you do not waste money on unnecessary things and you do not need to eliminate clutter from your home so frequently anymore.

Look atthe Positive Side of Things

As you go about the process of decluttering, it can be easy to see it as a hassle or feel guilty or upset about the things that you are eliminating. You may attempt to justify them or barter with yourself to talk yourself into keeping them because you feel so guilty about purchasing something that ended up being wasteful in the end. This type of mentality can be further amplified by a negative mindset along the way. Taking your time to focus on your mindset and using this as an opportunity to really consider your thought processes is a great opportunity for you to ensure that you are looking on the bright side of things and making the most out of the situation.

Instead of seeing the experience as being negative or embarrassing, embrace it as a learning experience and a moment of growth. Choose to celebrate yourself for the massive changes that you are making towards experiencing a more positive future, and really embody those feelings of celebration and joy. The more you look at the bright side of things and see all of the positives that you are gaining from your decluttering, the better the process will feel in general.

Begin Building More Positivity into Your Life

As you move through the process of decluttering your life, do not wait to begin building more positive practices into it. There is no reason for you to put off your new positive experiences until you reach a certain point of your decluttering process or until you have fully completed it. In fact, that is actually not advisable as making yourself wait can only make the process of decluttering even harder. When you make yourself wait unnecessarily, you prevent yourself from seeing the value of the experience and you end up feeling as though it is pointless since you are not gaining any rewards from your efforts. Instead, start building new positive experiences into your life right away. As you declutter your mind, start infusing your life with a more positive practice that you genuinely enjoy, such as singing or laughing more. As you declutter your home, invest in doing more of what you enjoy since you no longer have to stress over the cleaning that needs to be done. As you declutter your relationships and finances, start going out more and doing more positive things (within your means) with the people whom you care about.

The sooner you begin infusing your life with the positive rewards of your practice, the sooner you will be able to genuinely enjoy your life. You will also start finding that the rewards of your decluttering practice are so great that it makes it far more meaningful and worthwhile in the long run. Giving yourself a greater opportunity to focus on the positive aspects of your life will keep you motivated and moving forward, making it easier for you to continue living a continually happier life.

Conclusion

Congratulations on completing *Declutter!*

I hope that this book was effective in helping you understand the power of decluttering, the best methods for doing so, and healthy habits you can pick up along the way to ensure that you are maintaining a healthy sense of wellbeing as you go. Decluttering can be one of the most rewarding experiences there is, but it can also be one of the most trying experiences. As you go through a lifetime of belongings, memories, and emotions, it can be exhausting and overwhelming to face everything. Remember, you do not have to rush the experience and you are always able to ask for help and rely on support to get you through the process. Be reasonable with your expectations and work at a pace that serves you, not one that leads to you experiencing feelings of shock and overwhelm.

As you move forward after the process of decluttering, I strongly encourage you to continue practicing every single step in this book along the way. Just because you have successfully decluttered does not mean that the clutter cannot sneak back in through unexpected means. By paying close attention to your habits and keeping an eye on your life and home, you can ensure that clutter has nowhere to accumulate and that it does not take over again. That way, you can maintain the positive and happy benefits of the decluttering process and avoid reverting back into the stress and chaos of having clutter in your life.

Make sure that as you go, you stay open to learning and you continue to practice compassion and empathy towards yourself. It is not uncommon for people who are new to living a decluttered, minimalistic lifestyle to find themselves reverting back into old habits of accumulating clutter and letting it pile up. Simply notice any time you see this happening and take the necessary action to create a solution and eliminate the clutter once again. As you continue reinforcing your new habits and practices, you will find that maintaining a clean and clutter-free life will become significantly easier for you.

Lastly, I hope that you find many great joys and blessings in your new clutter-free life! Thank you so much for reading this book.

If you've enjoyed this book, I would appreciate it if you went to the place of purchase and left a short positive review. Thank you

www.ingramcontent.com/pod-product-compliance
Lightning Source LLC
Chambersburg PA
CBHW020547080526
44583CB00013B/1041